The Least of My People

Poetry by Dianna Jennings

DORRANCE
PUBLISHING CO
EST. 1920
PITTSBURGH, PENNSYLVANIA 15238

Dorrance Publishing Co
585 Alpha Drive
Suite 103
Pittsburgh, PA 15238
Visit our website at *www.dorrancebookstore.com*

ISBN: 979-8-88683-647-9
eISBN: 979-8-88683-648-6

The Least of My People

The Least of My People

When I closed my eyes all I could see

Was that sweet frightened face beneath a coward's knee

Don't tell me what matters, I've seen how it's been

For folks with an accent or dark colored skin

And don't get me wrong, there are lots of good cops

But they're at risk too until this racism stops.

When I turned my eyes back to what I did not want to see

My blurred eyes saw Jesus then under that knee

And I heard these words as clear as can be

Whatsoever you do unto the least of my people, so also you do

unto me.

Take Me Out Coach

Take me out coach I'm weary I can't play any more

You've used up all I have to give

I've nothing else in store

It's not the way it used to be

It doesn't feel the same

I find nothing to sustain me and

I hate this worthless game

Take me out coach and don't put me on the bench

Take away my jersey, take the locker key away

Call me what you want to but I'm never going to play

You atrophied my muscles, wrenched away my heart

Gave me only endings but promised me my start

Take me out coach make it the next play you call

I'll run right off this cursed field and never think of you at all.

The Dig

You cannot catalog me, dust off my bones
And number where I'm found.
I am the eyes that stare out from empty sockets
The lips that give the warmth to
Dead bone grin.
I am the throat for whom those
Beads were strung
I am the flesh, the spoken word,
The outside chance.
Your eyes tumbled towards me like dice.
Carefully you glean all of me that you need
And brush the rest into the reddened sand.
Boxed up, labeled, stored, my nose pushed
Flat against the glass, pressing to be free
Your knees scraped from rugged rocks, eyes shot.
Bone by bone, straw by straw,
shard by shard
To piece me back together is to see
What the desert dust cannot erode.

An Accomplished Woman

Here's what I put in a box beneath my bed
To be opened by family and friends when I'm dead:
A log book proving I'd soloed a plane
Here I am boarding a Siberian train
Look at me here on Mongolia's steppes
That's me in Paris eating fresh crepes
I'm throwing a boomerang…hmm, quite adept
(You'll probably notice the figure I've kept!)
Ah how I enjoyed the Hermitage halls
And visiting the homeland of Romans and Gauls
Then paddling a kayak through San Juan's waters
And later, California, where I'm swimming with otters
I'm sixty in this one. I think that's Cancun
This one's in Turkey, some Pasha's plush room.
Box of my wonders for all to discern…
I strike up the match and watch it all burn.

MAMA

Mama, Mama, why's your face so white?

The machine quit breathing for you and you slipped into the night.

Mama, I'm so frightened let me sleep here by the light.

Turning, spinning wildly, rubber bodies piled high.

Limbo rocking to your stocking, pounding on your thigh

Take me with you, Mama, if you really mean to die.

There's no place left to hide in, Ma, there's no place left with heat

Just that icy stare of death that strips your bones and rots your meat.

God, won't somebody help me put the flesh back on her feet!

I know it wasn't personal when you squeezed me from your womb

And I should take it like a trooper as they drop you down that tomb

But God, it's lonely Mama sitting back here in this room.

Well, he really didn't know you and he didn't know me much

And I knew before I married him, he'd resent it if I clutch

But I cried like a little baby Ma, for the comfort of his touch

For the comfort of some touching, Ma or a tender look and maybe

If he'd stretched his arms out to me, I'd not be crying here like a baby.

Crying like a baby, Mama, crying like a kid

For what you did by dying

And for the things he never did.

I'm pounding on my chest, Ma, my thoughts are mad and wild

I'm crying like a baby, like a baby, like your baby, I'm crying like

A baby Ma, like your precious little child.

The Workshop

I can see into you as if you are made of glass
Like the jars holding nails and screws
In the old man's workshop.
You are covered with the same dust and it ages you.
You are the hobby and the hobby is repetition
Repetition without novelty
The hammer strikes, lifts, strikes, lifts...bang, bang, bang.

The Confessional

Sneaking into the confessional
I'd hold together with trembling fingers
The heavy mourning curtain
That kept me incognito.
Waiting, with no possible way of undetected escape,
I'd columnize my errors
Gray venials on one side,
Black mortals on the other
And I'd keep score
Indulgence for indulgence
Until the tiny window opened
s-w-i-s-h
like a falling guillotine!

Bearing

My belly stretched and thin scars zipped across it
Like stubbed chalk on a black board.
For seven months I never slept upon my back
For fear my spine would be too rugged of a pallet for your tiny bones
No more prepared for bearing than for dying when those walls that
Had protected you puckered violently and pushed you from my guts
Stinking, bleeding son severed from me in the stupor of birth
So that later in the rapture of affection I could not reel you back
into my womb.
Through angled mirrors I watched the medic's hands...knit and
purl, knit and purl
I awoke to find my navel had come loose and dimpled once again
beneath my skin.

Covid Dream

In my dream you are there outside my window
I cup my hands around the sweetness of your face
Longing for the warmth of your countenance
But feel only the chill of damp glass

Love Song

I saw you last night again
In the twilight softness between
Consciousness and sleep
Gently your image came to me
And made me fight to stay awake a little longer.
Your face was so comfortable
I wanted to climb into it,
So warm it made me blush.
I carried you nestled closely against me
On the undulating journey into sleep
Hours later when the cobwebs cleared from my drowsy head
You were there still as the rush that warmed me and the joy
That filled me through all the day.

Comfort for the broken heart

Brooding won't answer your questions
And hiding won't settle your mind
And mathematics won't help you understand
The angst of all mankind
But something tender among the losses
Tucked into small pockets of yearning
Makes way through the doubts
In tiny amounts
To where love is once again burning.

Dragons Song

One by one on a red moon night

The dragons assembled awaiting first light

They scratched the ground and whipped their tails

And snapped at one another with claws sharp as nails

Then silently lifted up off the ground and flew off together to

never be found

Where are they now and why did they go?

Generations have sought them yet still we don't know.

Was it magic or hydra or some evil curse or mankind

And greed or something much worse that uprooted the dragons

that settled the earth

And sent them to hide in the metaverse?

Well, they had what we wanted, skin, riches and fire and our

standing among

Creatures was considerably higher.

They were good these dragons aggressive and yet they suffered and

were injured

Each time that we met. No respite, no chances, no options were good

They were wounded and weary and misunderstood

They were different, could fly and their breathe was on fire

Their skin was unholy, glowed green on the pyre

They all left on wing on a red moon dawn...

Oh my god, can't you see, it's our fault they are gone!

Ichythyosaur

Briny water covered this desert once and through it swam the
ichythyosaur breaking through the waves for air
We rode the road like waves, undulating. I sat close, drowning in
you and the wide Nevada landscape I think, perhaps, my hand
upon your thigh.
Ichythyosaur, with eyes the size of boulders sucking in ancient
mollusks where we now sucked in the silent tableau.
We found an empty cabin and spread our bags atop the singing
bed springs floating layers above where he once swam.
Now I read "their widespread existence and apparent success
makes their disappearance all the more Mysterious" and I wonder
where you went.

The Woman on Ward G

With volunteer-made slippers

Tied onto her bony feet

She shuffled along the corridors of Ward G

From locked door to locked door

Moaning "Jesus, won't ya gather up my clothes."

An old woman

With eyes sunk so deeply into the sockets

That from a distance only darkness could be seen.

Around her they laughed at her shuffling and moaning,

At her shrieking to her Jesus—

To her Jesus who

Had left her alone

Dying in a sterile gown

With slippers tied onto her feet

Had left her strapped to a bed at night

With rails so high that even he could not climb in to comfort her.

That shuffling is still in my ears

And her shrieking sticks with me

Like a banshee's wail.

Up and down in my mind I hear her

"Oh Jesus, won't ya gather up my clothes, dear Jesus.

Dear Jesus, won't ya

Gather up my clothes"

www.ingramcontent.com/pod-product-compliance
Lightning Source LLC
Chambersburg PA
CBHW072144150726
48002CB00004B/1627